GRAND UNION CANAL

GRAND UNION CANAL

IAN J. WILSON

TEMPUS

To my wife Jo

Frontispiece: A pair of narrowboats both with sidecloths drawn up in Apsley Top Lock (No.65) near Hemel Hempstead, probably between the two world wars. The motor boat is on the right with deck lid open, and the butty is on the left with forecabin. The slack towing rope hanging from the butty's topmast can be seen running along the top planks and through the running blocks towards the back cabin. The boatman and his wife are closing top gates and paddles, whilst their daughter makes her way past the lock cottage probably to open the paddles at bottom of lock. In the distance can be seen Durrants Hill Road Bridge No.152 and to the right of it is the Albion pub.

First published 2004

Tempus Publishing Limited
The Mill, Brimscombe Port,
Stroud, Gloucestershire, GL5 2QG
www.tempus-publishing.com

British Library Cataloguing in Publication Data.
A catalogue record for this book is available from the British Library.

ISBN 0 7524 2933 7

Typesetting and origination by Tempus Publishing Limited.
Printed in Great Britain by Midway Colour Print, Wiltshire.

Contents

Acknowledgements

All the illustrations used in this publication are taken from my own collection of postcards and photographs; any credits due have been made alongside each photograph. The pictures have been arranged topographically from the south (Brentford) to the north (Braunston) and branches or arms from their junction with the main line to their terminus (except the Paddington Arm). This publication does not cover canals that were acquired at a later date by the Grand Junction Canal Co. such as the section of canal we now refer to as the Leicester Line of the Grand Union Canal, mainly because I have virtually no postcards in my collection of this part of the system and none of the Northampton Arm, neither old nor new. This is not to say that none exist, but I have found none for my collection and was unable to borrow any from other collectors whilst compiling this book.

I served for nearly twenty years on the committee of the Grand Union Canal Society, some of that time as Chairman. I have also boated and walked the towpaths along most of the old Grand Junction Canal for many years and therefore it is mostly my own accumulated knowledge that has helped me compile the information about this collection of photographs. However, I would like to thank Alan Faulkner, whose various written histories of this canal have been a reliable source for me to check my facts against.

The following have also given assistance: David Blagrove, Avril Lansdell, Philip Griffiths, Tony Collins (Buckingham Canal Society), plus many of my colleagues in the Canal Card Collectors Circle.

I would like to thank both J. Salmon & Son and Judges Ltd for allowing me to use some of their postcard images in this publication. I am grateful to Alex Prowse and Garth Allan for allowing me to use some of their drawings that had been published on postcards, and to Martin Wood for allowing me to use several of his photographs.

Introduction

The Act of Parliament for the construction of the Grand Junction Canal was given Royal Assent on 30 April 1793; construction work commenced on the main line between Brentford and Braunston in May of the same year.

Three years earlier in 1790 a waterway route had been completed between London and Birmingham via Oxford, using the River Thames and Oxford Canal. Despite the Oxford Canal being narrow with a long circuitous route and the Thames still being reliant on old style flash locks, trade developed rapidly.

Unlike the narrow Oxford Canal, the Grand Junction was built as a wide barge canal, with wide locks and a much straighter, and therefore more direct, route to Oxford Canal at Braunston. From its commencement in 1793 to its completion in 1805, the Grand Junction Canal's construction caused its engineers William Jessop and James Barnes numerous problems. Two big tunnels had to be cut at Blisworth (3,056 yards long) and Braunston (2,048 yards long), embankments and aqueducts built at Cosgrove and Weedon, plus a long cutting through the Chiltern Hills at Tring. Provision of regular water supplies to the summits at Tring and Braunston were also a major challenge involving much construction work. By late 1800, construction was complete, except for the tunnel at Blisworth and the crossing of the Great Ouse at Cosgrove.

Various branch canals were authorised within the first and subsequent Grand Junction Canal Acts, permitting the company to build branches to Paddington (opened 1801), Slough (1882), Wendover (1799), Aylesbury (1815), Old Stratford (1800), Buckingham (1801) and Northampton (1815) which made a connection with the River Nene in Northampton. A short section of the River Chess at Batchworth was canalised in 1805. A number of extended docks were constructed on the main line and Paddington Arm, especially in the Southall and Hayes area of Middlesex to the west of London.

An independent company promoted and built a branch to Newport Pagnell in 1817, which survived until 1864 when it was bought out by the Newport Pagnell Railway Co. (not covered in this publication).

Although the main line of the canal was built to a wide beam there was some variation when it came to the branches.

Paddington	13 Miles 4 Furlongs	Level	14ft beam
Slough	4 Miles 7 Furlongs	Level	14ft beam
Wendover	6 Miles 6 Furlongs	Level (with Stop Lock)	14ft beam
Aylesbury	6 Miles 2 Furlongs	16 Locks	7ft beam
Old Stratford	1 Mile 2 Furlongs	Level	14ft beam
Buckingham	9 Miles 4 Furlongs	2 Locks	7ft beam
Northampton	4 Miles 6 Furlongs	17 Locks	7ft beam
Rickmansworth (River Chess)	2 Furlongs	1 Lock	14ft beam

The Grand Union Canal Co. was formed by the amalgamation which came into force on 1 January 1929, of the first eight named undertakings below, which were thus brought under unified control, covering the route between London, Birmingham and Leicester. The three last mentioned waterways were acquired from 1 January 1932 and extended the existing routes to further centres of production in Leicestershire, Nottinghamshire and Derbyshire.

The names of the constituent canals and the years in which they originated are as follows:

1. Grand Junction Canal	1793
2. Leicestershire & Northamptonshire Canal	1793
3. Warwick & Birmingham Canal	1793
4. Warwick & Napton Canal	1794
5. Grand Union Canal	1810
6. Regent's Canal	1812
7. Hertford Union Canal	1824
8. Birmingham & Warwick Junction Canal	1840
9. Loughborough Navigation	1776
10. Erewash Canal	1777
11. Leicester Navigation	1799

The fact that the industrial centre of Britain developed around Birmingham and the Black Country meant that raw products were carried along the canal to the Midlands with the finished products carried back towards London and south-east England. This changed in time as companies grew up along the route of the canal. Some companies like John Dickenson's, the paper manufacturer at Apsley in Hertfordshire, were there before the canal was built, situated alongside the River Gade.

All the major canal carriers used the Grand Junction whilst it was still being used as a commercial waterway, and some of these can be seen at work in the pictures within this publication.

Ian J. Wilson
December 2003

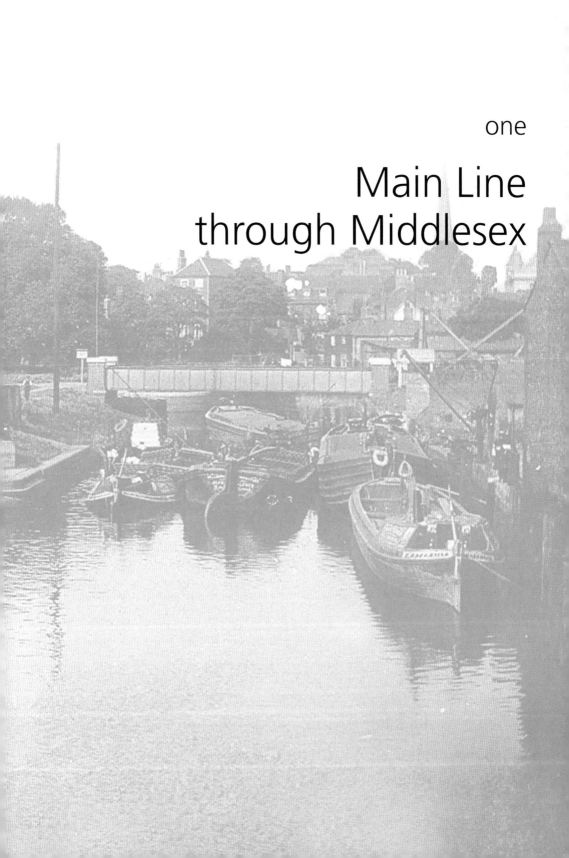

one

Main Line
through Middlesex

The postage stamp was issued in 1993 to celebrate the bicentenary of the passing of the Act of Parliament to commence building the Grand Junction Canal. (A.J. Lewery – Royal Mail 1993)

Painting showing the Ham where the river Brent and the canal flow along the same course below Brentford High Street, Middlesex. Many boats can be seen, along with the small cranes used to load and unload them. There are also wooden warehouses and the tower of St Lawrence's church (New Brentford) which is above trees and roof tops.

Brentford Gauging Locks (No.100) from Brentford High Street Bridge (No.209), *c*.1920. The southern terminus of the canal is close to its junction with the river Thames and was always a busy point. There is a variety of craft in this picture, including many narrowboats, lighters and also a transom stern barge to the right in the river Brent. The bridge crossing the river Brent carries the access road to Brentford Depot which is on an island between the canal and river. The small building to the left of the locks is the Fellows, Morton & Clayton office, and the building on the right is the Grand Junction toll office.

Brentford Gauging Locks after record rainfall in June 1903. The view looks toward Brentford Depot and is probably taken from the footbridge over the tail of locks shown in the top picture on page 11. The canal above the lock turns round to the left before the moored lighters. Brentford was often subject to flooding as this lower section of the Grand Junction Canal was a canalised part of the river Brent, just above its junction with the river Thames.

Above: A line of barges moored against the island between the canal and the river Brent, Grand Junction Canal at Brentford, *c.*1920. A number of narrowboats are moored behind barges with children standing on the cabin roofs. In the distance the bridge that carries the Hounslow Loop Line railway can be seen.

Right: London United Tramways poster showing a narrowboat probably approaching New Brentford/Clitheroes Lock (No.99) on the lower reaches of the Grand Junction Canal. In many places along the lower reaches the river frequently flows in and out of the canal. (Paul Rieth 1914 – London Transport Museum)

RIVER BRENT BY TRAM

Willow Wren motor boat *Curlew* heading up the canal just above New Brentford/Clitheroes Lock and just below Gallows Bridge (No.207). The taut towrope suggests the motor is towing a butty out of picture. In the background above the trees the elevated section of the M4 motorway is visible. Another picture of *Curlew* is on page 68. (J. Salmon Ltd)

A pair of Fellows, Morton & Clayton narrowboats, the steamer *Sultan* (launched 1899) with butty *Ash* in tow, near New Brentford Lock, *c.*1905. A post with a semaphore signal is behind the boats on the horizon, beside the Brentford Docks branch of the GWR.

Above: Three Bridges, Hanwell, *c.*1910. A bridge already carried Windmill Lane over the canal before Isambard Kingdom Brunel planned to take the Brentford Docks branch of the Great Western Railway through a cutting under both canal and road. Designed in 1859, Three Bridges is actually two bridges, with road, rail and canal routes intersecting at different angles on three levels. The massive brick arches at low level can be clearly seen in this photograph, as well as the 'trough' supported by huge metal beams to carry the road above the canal. Several people are peering over the parapet of the road bridge, and there are also a couple of boatmen holding onto the tillers of their boats. Although it is now single tracked, the railway is still used by waste transfer trains. Three Bridges along with the Hanwell Flight of Locks is now a scheduled ancient monument.

Opposite above: Below Lock No.97 at the bottom of Hanwell Flight, *c.*1906, looking south towards Osterley and Brentford. The bridge on the left takes the canal towpath over the river Brent, which flows into the canal at this point. Below the bridge by the towpath there appears to be a street lamp. In the distance are the rooftops of the Victorian terraces that are still there today.

Opposite below: A pair of T.& D. Murrell's boats entering Lock No.96 on Hanwell Flight in February 1979. The butty *Bude* and motor *Towcester* are loaded with about 50 tons of lime juice barrels for L. Rose & Co. at Boxmoor Wharf, Hemel Hempstead. This was one of the last regular commercial runs on the canal. Snow is lying on the ground, and in the distance some of the buildings belonging to the St Bernard's Asylum, Hanwell, can be seen. The picture on the bottom of page 44 is of the same two boats unloading at Boxmoor Wharf. (Beric Tempest)

Grand Junction Canal at Southall Mill by J.M.W. Turner, 1806. Turner's drawing for this painting is said to have been made one evening on his way from visiting a friend at Heston. The road that now crosses the Three Bridges Aqueduct at Hanwell is called Windmill Lane. It probably takes its name from this mill, which was situated at Norwood Green. The lock shown in the painting is either the top lock of the Hanwell Flight or Norwood Bottom Lock. Two figures are pushing balance beams to close the bottom gates. There is a white horse standing below the wing wall of the lock, and there is a canal bridge in the distance. (Christie's Images, London/Bridgeman Art Library)

Norwood Top Lock (No.90), Southall, c.1920. Beyond the tail of the lock is a whitewashed bridge No.204 that carries Glade Lane over the canal. The bottom gates of the lock are open, with the lock keeper standing outside an attractive-looking lock cottage, and another figure in front of a telegraph pole. The mooring bollards are of the large wooden type. Each top gate has a pair of gate paddles plus a ground paddle on each side of the lock. On the right of the lock is a paddle gear, which was possibly for a side pond. The pond is no longer there, and is now the site of a British Waterways yard.

Norwood Top Lock, Southall, *c*.1960, a reverse view of the previous picture, but taken forty years later from Glade Lane Bridge. The lock number has been hand painted on the right-hand balance beam, and there is water pouring over the bottom gates. The lock cottage has had its walls rendered, and hardly looks like the attractive cottage in the previous picture; however, the paddles and bollards are the same. In the distance beyond the lock, several barges are moored by the entrance to the Maypole Dock which is on the right. The Maypole Dock was built in 1914 to serve Otto Monsted's margarine works.

Wolf Bridge, Norwood Green, Southall, *c*.1900. The buildings behind the bridge on the towpath side are part of Norwood flour mill, the first factory in this area, originally steam powered. The mill was destroyed by fire in 1912. The area on the left of the canal where the wooden fence, shed and large tree are situated, is now the garden of The Lamb public house. Just to the left of the garden on the edge of the picture, is the back cabin and part of a well-laden narrowboat. The picture at the top of page 18 was taken from this bridge, and shows the view beyond.

THE CANAL, SOUTHALL

Above: View from Wolf Bridge looking west, at Norwood Green, Southall, *c.*1930. A heavily laden barge is being pulled by a horse. Two men are on the rear of the barge, the right being the steerer. A third man in the middle distance is leading the horse along the towing path. The buildings along the towpath that were originally part of Norwood flour mill were by this time in use as a picture-framing factory, and later as a boys' hostel. Often the type of barge in this picture would be towed up the Thames from London Docks by tug into the canal at Brentford. Usually the cargoes would be transhipped into narrowboats at Brentford Depot, but quite a few barges would continue their journey up the Grand Junction Canal, sometimes as far as Berkhamsted in the Chilterns.

Opposite above: Canal Side, near North Hyde, Southall, *c.*1900. A group of children are standing by a towpath bridge, which is probably over the entrance to Adelaide Dock. The dock was originally built in 1850 for use by Norwood flour mill, and later by Southall/Norwood UDC. It is still open, and was until recently the base for a boat hire company. The trees along the left are in the grounds of Norwood Court, built by Josiah Wedgwood.

Opposite below: Probably a reverse of the previous view, Canal Side, near North Hyde, Southall, *c.*1900. There were originally two docks along this section of the Grand Junction Canal. This is possibly Victoria dock which was built for use by Sanders tube works and was closed and filled in many years ago. The towpath bridge has been blocked off by a barrier, and the towpath runs across the dock at ground level, where several men are sitting and children playing. The house in the distance with a pitched roof and chimney can be seen from the other side in the picture above.

Canal Side, Southall

CANAL SIDE, SOUTHALL.

Painting showing bridge No.201 which now carries Western Road, North Hyde, Middlesex. In a very rural setting, a man looks over the parapet of the bridge and a couple walk past the Grand Junction Arms public house, which proudly advertises 'Reids Stout'. There is a gas lamp by the bridge and the top of another can be seen in the distance.

Looking east, not far from Bull's Bridge Junction, Canal Side, North Hyde, Southall, c.1900. Once again a group of children are standing on the towpath. This is the same bridge shown above; it was rebuilt in 1930 with a flat deck. The Grand Junction Arms cannot be seen in this view as it lies back from the towpath and is hidden by the row of cottages. A narrowboat is moored near the bridge with two men on the bank next to it.

Canal and Hayes Cocoa Coy's Factory.

Hayes Cocoa Co.'s factory and canal, *c.*1930. On the back of this postcard the writer mentions that the factory is now operated by Nestlé. The view looks east where the far-off bridge carries the Great Western Railway main line from Paddington. The narrowboat on the canal appears to be bow hauled by the two men on the towpath. Coal brought from the Cannock Colliery by pairs of Willow Wren boats was still delivered to Nestlé by canal until 1958.

Canal Bridge. Hayes

Station Road Bridge (No.200), Hayes. *c.*1920. This bridge was modernised and rebuilt in 1934. A group of men including the local policeman are standing on the bridge To the right of the bridge parapet is a post with a diamond-shaped weight restriction sign. There is also a well worn track on the offside of the canal bank, which is probably a local short cut. The roof tops and chimneys of buildings in Silverdale Road can be seen behind the bridge.

Canal Bridge, Yiewsley

Above: Cowley Lock, Uxbridge, *c.*1910. A Fellows, Morton & Clayton motor has just entered Cowley Lock (No.89) towing the butty *Oak*. The boatwoman wearing a bonnet is at the tiller of the butty. The towrope from the motor is passing through the running blocks on the top planks of the butty. Beyond the lock is Cowley Bridge, which carries Iver Lane over the canal. The Frays River is a man-made diversion of the river Colne, built to supply the local millers with water. At this point the river passes underneath the lock. Originally one of the cottages on the right of the lock was for the Canal Co.'s lock keeper, and the other for the Duke of Northumberland's Inspector, who monitored the water on behalf of the millers.

Opposite above: Colham Bridge, Yiewsley, 1905. This bridge was rebuilt at a later date as, can be seen in the picture below. An empty narrowboat is moored beyond the bridge on the offside of the picture. The large building to the left of the bridge is probably a flour mill, as there were several in this locality. The sign painted on the wall by the canal states – 'Good Mixing Flour' with a finger pointing towards the bridge or mill.

Opposite below: Colham Bridge, Yiewsley, *c.*1940. This rebuilt bridge is still in place today, but now looks a little dirtier than on this picture. A couple of boys are fishing on the canal towpath, and three men are peering over the bridge parapet. The large mill building still stands but has obviously had some minor modifications carried out since the previous picture was taken. The area on the nearside of the bridge is now covered with trees and shrubs.

View from above Cowley Lock, *c.*1950. There is a cottage on the left behind the towpath wall. A horse stands on the towpath feeding from his nose bowl. The slack towing rope can be seen trailing on the ground behind the horse. Two men stand by the top gates, one on each side of the lock, patiently waiting for the lock to fill.

The Shovel Inn, Cowley. This pleasant canal side public house is situated above Cowley Lock. It takes its name from the navvies who dug the canal by hand using shovels. The inn is always a busy place, especially on a warm day. At this point the towpath changes sides, but is just out of picture. The end of Cowley bridge parapet can just be seen in the left corner. (Halcyon of Bushey)

The canal at Uxbridge, below Uxbridgr Lock, with a man fishing in the foreground, c.1947. The large barge on the right is loaded with timber, probably for Osborne, Stevens Timber Yard which was alongside the canal, just below this point. Another fisherman and a group of children are beyond the front of the barge on the towpath side. The distant bridge No.183 was last rebuilt in 1938, and carried the High Street and Oxford Road. Beyond the bridge more laden timber barges are moored.

Uxbridge Lock (No.88), c.1960. A pair of Blue Line Boats are breasted up and are passing under bridge No.184 and into Uxbridge Lock. Ernie Kendall is steering the motor *Roger* on the left, and Rose Bray is at the tiller of the butty *Raymond*. The roof and chimneys of Uxbridge Lock Cottage are above the parapet of the bridge. Another picture of the motor *Roger* is on page 59. (J. Salmon Ltd)

Above: Uxbridge Lock, *c.*1900. The top gates of the lock are open as a heavily laden narrowboat with steerer is about to leave the lock. A towing rope can just be seen leading from the foremast to the horse who is still busy feeding from his nose bowl. The boatwoman with a shawl wrapped around her head prepares to lead the horse along the towpath. Two boys on the towpath have nothing to do with the boat, but are just on their way to or from school. An empty widebeam narrowboat is above the lock on the right, and behind this is a house and buildings that belong to King's Mill. There are several figures standing on the bridge, including the policeman. It is not easy to see in this picture, but the balance beams on the bottom gates of Uxbridge Lock are short and stubby, because of the close proximity of the bridge over the tail of the lock. Full length balance beams would not have room to clear the brickwork of the bridge.

Opposite above: Denham Deep Lock (No.87), *c.*1910. A Fellows, Morton & Clayton butty enters the lock, with a boatwoman at the tiller, and a boatman standing alongside the right-hand bottom gate. The boat horse is further behind him. There are a lot of building materials lying around on the ground and beside the lock cottage, as though some construction work has recently taken place. This lock has a fall of 11.1in which is the deepest on the Grand Junction Canal. Because of this, it is one of the few locks still to retain its gate paddles. Immediately above the lock is a brick-built aqueduct taking the canal over the man-made Fray's River, which is why this lock is so deep.

Opposite below: Denham Deep Lock, 1987. A Leeds & Liverpool short boat, *Farnworth,* is converted into a trip boat for Colne Valley Passenger Boat Services. It waits above the lock whilst a pair of northbound working boats leave lock. At the time of this picture *Farnworth* was owned and worked by Murrell's, who had the cargo hold covered and seats added for the passengers. (Beric Tempest)

Above: Black Jack's Lock (No.85), Harefield, *c*.1940. This is the view south from above the lock, and Bridge No.178 is over the tail of the lock. This lock has never had a lock cottage, the one on the left being Gardners Cottage. Past tenants of the cottage have included Ann Todd, the actress, and Mr Leslie Mitchell, novelist and BBC commentator. The origin of this lock's name is obscure, and many legends have grown up around it. A past owner was a Negro, accredited with such a powerful physique that he could jump the 15in span of the lock with ease, and who was suspected of stealing windlasses from canal barges, before being murdered by an irate victim. His ghost is said to haunt the area of the lock, hence the custom of 'no moorings hereabouts at night!'

Opposite above: Ruislip reservoir, near Northwood, Middlesex, 1908. The reservoir which covered 77 acres was originally built by Grand Junction Canal Co. in 1810, and supplied water to the main line near Norwood top lock. A new feeder was built later and the water was supplied to Paddington Arm. In the foreground there are a couple of punts, and to the left of the large tree there is the roof of a cottage with a chimney.

Opposite below: Ruislip reservoir, Middlesex, *c*.1920. This reservoir was eventually no longer required by the canal company, which converted it into a water sports area. In 1951 it was sold by the British Transport Commission to Northwood – Ruislip UDC, and became Ruislip Lido, a large water skiing centre and swimming area. As in the previous picture, several boats are moored on the reservoir with one against the bank in the foreground.

Ruislip Reservoir nr. Northwood.

32116 RUISLIP RESERVOIR.

Springwell Lock, Harefield, *c.*1910. Bridge No.176 carries Springwell Lane over the canal at this point. Behind the bridge, Springwell lock has steps leading up from the towpath to the top of the lock chamber. Two empty narrowboats are moored on the right. Here, the wharf was used to load boats with chalk and gravel from quarries in the Harefield Hillside. Chalk and gravel were brought down to this wharf by way of Springwell Lane and a small tramway.

Grand Junction Canal near the Middlesex Hertfordshire border, between Stockers Lock and Rickmansworth, 1948. A loaded horse-drawn gravel barge heads north towards Rickmansworth. A woman walks along the towpath with a man in front of her, alongside a horse which is towing the barge. The steerer stands in the stern of the barge, holding the tiller. The tops of mounds of gravel can be seen in the hold of the barge.

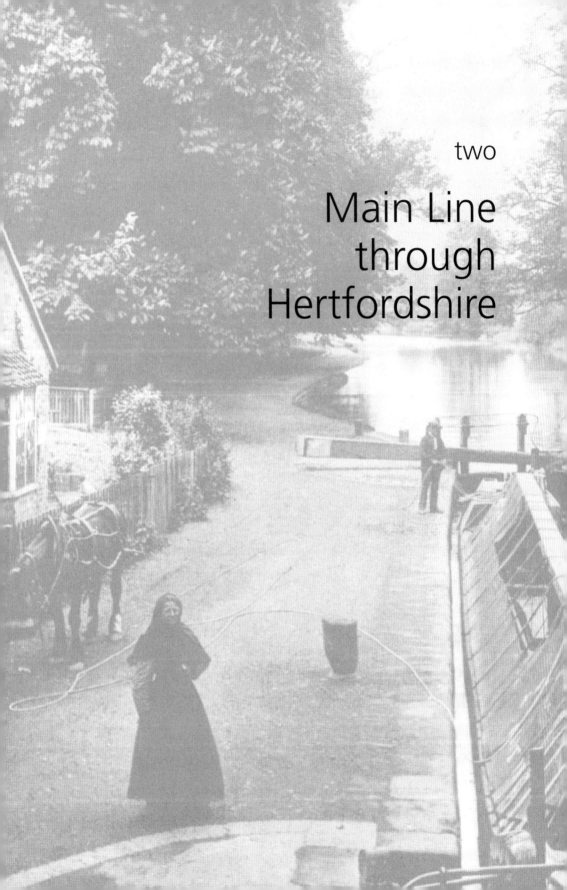

two

Main Line through Hertfordshire

Grand Junction Canal at Batchworth, Rickmansworth, *c*.1950. From Batchworth Bridge No.173, this view looks south. The handrail on the left runs alongside the steps down to the towpath. The towpath bridge over river Colne is in the centre of the picture, and to the right of that, between the gap in the trees is part of the aquadrome. The buildings in front of the trees on the left were part of the wharf on an island between the river and the canal.

Batchworth Bridge, Rickmansworth, *c*.1920. The wooden building on the towpath side used to be stables. There is a small crane, and behind this a public house on the opposite side of road. A number of buildings on the right were part of a corn mill with its own wharf. This is a reverse view of the above view, but is taken at an earlier date. Apart from the canal and lock which can be seen beyond the bridge hole, all these buildings have been demolished, and the bridge has been rebuilt with a flat deck.

Batchworth Lock, Rickmansworth, *c*.1920. A pair of empty, breasted up, narrowboats are leaving the lock. Towing rope can be seen running from the boat's topmast, and a boatman is walking back along the gunwale of the other boat. The towpath bridge on the left is over the entrance lock to the Rickmansworth Arm (part of the river Chess), which was originally navigable to the town wharf. The roof which can be seen on the left belongs to Rickmansworth Arm lock cottage, which no longer exists. The lock cottage of the main lock has been rebuilt.

Batchworth Lock, Rickmansworth, *c*.1910. This card shows an identical view to the previous picture but was taken at a slightly earlier date. A pair of loaded narrowboats are leaving the lock, and once again a towrope can be seen running from the topmast of the front boat. Side cloths are half drawn up, and both boats also have fore cabins. A blurred image of a woman can be seen at the foot of the steps on the right. One of the top gates of the Rickmansworth Arm lock is open with the paddle drawn. More of the lock cottage can be seen than in previous picture, as the hedgerow has been cut lower.

Common Moor Lock (No.79), Croxley Green. This is a modern scene looking towards Watford, which shows the lock after it was rebuilt in 1998. It was rebuilt because a leaking culvert had caused one of the lock walls to tilt inwards, making the lock only partially operable. Thirty years ago, the huge Esparto grass sheds, which were part of Dickinson's Croxley mills, were along the right side of the image by the hedge and large tree. Coal was delivered to the mills by narrowboats until 1970. After closure the mills were demolished, and there is now no sign of what was once there. (Paul Bradley – Croxley Camera Club)

Opposite above: Lifting bridge, Rickmansworth Arm (river Chess), c.1990. The restored narrowboat *Aldgate* in Colne Valley Carriers livery is passing beneath a lift bridge to gain access to Church Wharf and basin, which are still used today as moorings for boats. (Gulielma Publications)

Above: Ironbridge, No.167, Cassiobury Park, Watford. This ink drawing by Alex Prowse shows a scene that has changed very little over several hundred years. The name is misleading; the 'Ironbridge' referred to crosses the adjacent River Gade. (A.R. Prowse)

Right: Ironbridge and Lock, Cassiobury Park, Watford, c.1940. This photograph shows the same view as the previous picture, including the huge trees that grow in the park and alongside the canal. This white washed bridge is a little different than most traditional canal bridges: the parapet is flat, and rises to a point, as does the arch beneath, which curves to a point. The lock can be seen through the bridgehole.

Ironbridge Lock, Cassiobury Park, Watford, 1908. This is an empty lock with top gates open and paddles drawn. The lock cottage did not belong to the Grand Junction Canal Co. but to the Earl of Essex. When his ancestral home, Cassiobury House, was demolished in 1927, so was the lock cottage.

Ironbridge Lock, Cassiobury Park, Watford, c.1910. There are a pair of horse drawn Fellows, Morton & Clayton boats; *Liverpool* is in the lock and is followed by another entering the lock behind it. The horse by the lock cottage is eating out of his nose bowl with horse cloth covering him. The silhouette of the trees and their branches suggest this is a winter scene.

Ironbridge Lock, cottage and bridge, *c.*1910. The view is from the top of the lock looking towards the cottage and bridge. The top gates are open, both pairs of gate paddles and both ground paddles are drawn, and the lock is full as if a boat is expected. From this angle it gives a better idea of the full extent of the lock cottage. There is also a large wooden bollard in the foreground at the lockside.

Grand Junction Canal, Cassiobury Park, Watford, 1915. This picture shows the canal a little away above Ironbridge Lock, with a northbound boat in middle distance. The image depicts a good view of this large area of parkland with plenty of trees and open spaces.

The Lock, Cassiobury Park, Watford.

Above: Ironbridge Lock, Cassiobury Park, Watford, *c.*1909. A busy scene shows a pair of Fellows, Morton & Clayton horse-drawn boats in the lock. Both boats are sheeted up, and the one on the left has a forecabin. A boatman is standing near the top gates, with a boatwoman in the foreground wearing a long skirt and shawl around her head. They are both patiently waiting for the lock to empty. Meanwhile, the horse is beside the lock cottage, quietly eating from his nosebowl. The slack towropes can be seen hanging from the topmasts of both boats, and trailing along the ground behind the bollard, the boatwoman and around the horse's feet.

Opposite above: Cassiobury Park Top Lock (No.75), Watford. 1925. This is a picture from below this lock, which only has a fall of 4ft.6in, but which has plenty of water pouring over the bottom gates. Turnover bridge No.166 is above the lock, and takes the towpath over to the east side of the canal. Originally this would have been near the boundary between the The Grove, the Earl of Clarendon's estate, and Cassiobury Park owned by the Earl of Essex.

Opposite below: Ornamental Bridge at The Grove, Watford. The postcard is an ink drawing by Alex Prowse. When the Earl of Clarendon, who was a shareholder in the canal company, allowed the Grand Junction Canal to be constructed through his estate at Grove Park, he was paid £5,000 compensation for this inconvenience. The Earl also requested that this Ornamental Bridge be constructed over the canal to carry the driveway to his home and estate, Grove Park.
(Alex Prowse)

GROVE MILL LOCK. WATFORD.

Above: Unconverted narrowboat *Hadley Rail* near The Grove, Watford, in May 1985. The steerer in this view is Eily Gayford who was eighty-two. She was invited on the trip by John Evans, after giving the Grand Union Canal Society a talk about her experiences training boatwomen during the Second World War. This boat was a Large Woolwich, which was all steel. Built in 1937 by Harland & Wolff for Grand Union Canal Carrying Co, it was a 'Town' Class boat called *Hadley*. Later Willow Wren renamed her *Rail*. The owners at the time of this picture carried both her previous names. (Photograph by Martin Wood)

Opposite above: Hunton Bridge, 1915. A pair of horse-drawn narrowboats have just left Hunton Bridge Bottom Lock and are making the turn to pass under the old A41 road bridge. Both boats are sheeted up; the leading boat has a forecabin and has a towrope leading from its topmast. The river Gade can be seen flowing into the canal behind the second boat. In front of the cottage, immediately left of the river, is the back cabin of a narrowboat. It had been waiting for these two boats to leave the lock, so it could then enter.

Opposite below: Hunton Bridge, *c.*1960. A pair of empty Samuel Barlow coal boats are about to enter Hunton Bridge Bottom Lock (No.73). They are breasted up; *Cairo* is the motor on the left with a steerer, alongside the butty *Grace*. Men are fishing from the towpath on the left. The far-off white house above the lock is the cottage for Hunton Bridge Top Lock. There is a large barge moored to the right, close to the cottage seen in the previous picture. This picture has been taken from further along the right side than the previous one above, probably so that the locks could be seen. (J. Salmon Ltd)

The Lock, Apsley End

54369

The Paper Mills, Apsley End

Above: John Dickinson's paper mills at Apsley End, 1912. This picture shows Dickinson's powerhouse partly hidden by trees, which was superseded by a more modern powerhouse built in a different location in 1922. The canal runs across in the foreground. The white lock cottage for Apsley Bottom Lock (No.67) is to the left, opposite a small dock that leads towards the mill buildings. The whole of the area that was Dickinson's paper mills has recently been redeveloped, and replaced by residential accommodation built by Fairview Homes, along with a new marina and several new superstores.

Opposite above: Canal Weir at Kings Langley, *c.*1960. Along this section of Grand Junction Canal there are several weirs that take excess water from the canal, especially after spells of wet weather. The weirs discharge water into the adjacent river Gade, which accompanies the canal most of the way from Apsley down to Croxley.

Opposite below: Apsley Top Lock (No.65), 1908. Built in 1818, this was the top lock of the new canal line via Apsley and Nash Mills. Just behind the nearest telegraph pole was the entrance to Ebbern's Wharf, the original part of the old canal line. The Albion public house, which was demolished in 1998, is in centre distance. There is a full lock of water with top gates partly open. For another slightly later view see page 2.

Boxmoor, Hemel Hempstead, c.1910. This is possibly the view taken from Two Waters Bridge (No.151) looking towards Apsley. A pair of horse-drawn narrowboats are heading south. A white horse is partly hidden by a third telegraph pole, with a man walking on the towpath behind the horse. A boatman is at the tiller of the front boat, and the boatwoman is steering the second boat.

Boxmoor Wharf, Hemel Hempstead, c.1980. These are a pair of Murrell's boats. *Towcester* is on the left, alongside butty *Bude* which is unloading barrels of lime juice at L. Rose & Co.'s wharf, shortly before this traffic ceased. Two Waters Bridge is behind the boats. The picture on the bottom of page 14 shows the same two boats in Hanwell Flight on their way to Boxmoor. (Litho Productions)

Right: London General Omnibus Co. This poster shows a narrowboat with smoke drifting out of its cabin chimney, and a horse on the towpath pulling it along. A group of houses are in the distance. The poster advertises motor buses from Golders Green Station to Boxmoor. (Padden 1921 – London Transport Museum)

Below: Boxmoor Town Lock, 1911. A maintenance boat is moored on the towpath below the lock. A by-pass weir is to the right of the lock behind two boys fishing. It looks rather new and tidy as if it had been recently completed. The lock cottage disappeared many years ago. The small tower of St John's Church, Boxmoor, is on the right. The open area between the church and canal is now a cricket ground. The picture is possibly taken from a railway bridge that carried the branch line, which also closed many years ago, from Harpenden to Boxmoor.

BOXMOOR

BY MOTOR BUS ROUTE 146 FROM GOLDERS GREEN STATION

Moor and Canal, Boxmoor

Old Mill, Boxmoor

The Canal, Boxmoor

Above: Boxmoor, Hemel Hempstead, *c.*1910. This a reverse view of the one opposite. A pair of Fellows, Morton & Clayton boats are passing under Station Road Bridge, the front boat is a steamer; the steerer is wearing a white shirt with dark waistcoat, another crew member is stepping off onto the towpath under the bridge, probably to set up Town Lock which is a short distance ahead of them. The towing rope from the steamer is passing through the running blocks along the top planks of butty to the steerer, who has the tiller pushed out to the left ready for the turn under the bridge. The small tower of St John's Church, Boxmoor, can be seen, (see also page 45 bottom). The Grand Junction Canal Co. had to purchase 25 acres of the moor from the Boxmoor Trust, before the canal could be built.

Opposite above: Boxmoor, Hemel Hempstead, *c.*1910. This picture is taken from Station Road Bridge (No.150) looking north towards the Fishery Inn. There is an empty, possibly wide-beamed narrowboat with a towrope leading from the topmast. A horse is hidden in the dark shadows of the tall hedgerow running behind the towpath. The buildings and chimneys of Foster's Saw Mill are in the distance behind telegraph poles. To the right the path leads across the moor and has a few remote cottages.

Opposite below: Foster's saw mill, Boxmoor, Hemel Hempstead, 1908. A very heavily laden widebeam narrowboat carrying straw or hay is in the middle of the canal, opposite the tall mill building. The steerer is standing on the cabin roof so he can see where he is going. This mill was originally operated by Henry & Alfred Foster, who ran a boat of their own to supply the mill. The mill was burnt down but the chimney survived until it was demolished in 1969. A residential home was built on the site.

The Saw Mill, Boxmoor

Foster's saw mill, Boxmoor, Hemel Hempstead, *c*.1910. The mill is seen from the opposite direction of the previous picture. This view gives a better idea of the actual size of this saw mill. Some of the mill workers are standing alongside the wharf. At Bressingham Gardens and Steam Museum there is a Vernon & Guest single-cylinder horizontal mill engine brought from this mill at Boxmoor. It has a 12ft diameter flywheel which weighs 6 tons. The engine was restored and still steams.

Fishery Inn and Bridge, Boxmoor

Fishery Inn and bridge (No.149), Boxmoor, Hemel Hempstead. This postcard view may be a lot older than its posting date of 1948. Part of the large building beside the bridge with a small street lamp fixed to its corner, was originally a small general store. The rest of this building is part of the inn. The original stables were probably situated by the canal, below the over hanging bar room which carries the wording 'Fishery Inn'.

Fishery Lock (No.63), Boxmoor, Hemel Hempstead, *c*.1910. The same location as on page 48 is viewed from above Fishery Road Bridge (No.149). It appears as though a northbound boat has recently left lock, as it is full of water. The top gates are open and all paddles are drawn or open. In this picture you can see 'Austins' General Store attached to the end of The Fishery Inn, which is mentioned in the caption to the picture on page 50.

Boxmoor, Hemel Hempstead, *c*.1980. The passenger narrowboat *Kingfisher* of Tring is heading up the canal, during one of the Boxmoor boat rallies held during the 1970s and 1980s. Old Fishery Lane (No.148) in the background is no longer a through route as it used to be many years ago. Beyond the bridge, rows of moored boats are attending the rally. (Photo Precision Ltd)

Above: Fishery Inn & Lock, Boxmoor, Hemel Hempstead, *c*.1900. This is very similar to the view on p.49 (top) but busier, and a lack of shrubs behind the lock enables more to be seen in the background of this view. A pair of northbound boats are waiting to leave the lock, breasted up, with a man sitting on the top planks of nearest boat, with two men sitting on the balance beam of the top gate. All gate and ground paddles are drawn or open, and various towropes are trailing around in the foreground from the topmasts of both boats. Once again 'Austins' General Store is there. Both corners of the pub building have brackets fixed to the wall with lamps mounted upon them. The general store survived many years after this picture was taken, but when it eventually closed the 'Fishery Inn' extended into the space.

Opposite above: The Three Horseshoes pub and Winkwell Swing Bridge, Bourne End, *c*.1975. This swing bridge (No.147) across Winkwell Lane was operated by hand, which necessitated turning a large wheel many times. It was on the opposite side of the bridge outside the pub, and has now been converted to electric operation. On its outside wall, the Three Horseshoes states that it has been here since 1335. Beyond the bridge is Winkwell Top Lock (No.60).

Opposite below: A Samuel Barlow motor, *Admiral*, pulling a butty, possibly out of Bourne End Top Lock (No.56), 1948. Along the narrow strip at the top of the cabin side is the registration, 'No.524' at Daventry. Below the boat name *Admiral* is the Grand Union gauging number 'GU12157'. The double doors to the engine hole are open, showing the 'roses and castles' painted on the inside of the doors. It has a taller chimney, with brass rings and a deflector ring in the engine exhaust. There is an old oil lamp in front of the cabin above and the hold is full of coal. At the top of the embankment behind the canal is a competitor – coal wagons on the former LNWR main line. (H. C. Casserley/TWT)

CANAL, BERKHAMSTED.

Above: The Crystal Palace public house and Canal, Berkhamsted. *c* 1910. This is a very quiet scene, without a person to be seen or a boat on the move. The public house has its frontage dressed up to give the appearance of 'The Crystal Palace'. It also advertises 'Ivinghoe Fine Ales and Spirits' along its front. Castle Wharf is opposite the bank of the canal, and was owned up until this time by W.E. Costin Ltd. Boats and barges were built for many leading carriers at Castle Wharf. The yard closed around the time of this picture and was taken over by William Key & Son – Timber Merchants. A transom-sterned barge is moored by the wharf. A narrowboat cabin can be seen, but the rest of the boat is out of the picture. Berkhamsted Town Lock (No.54) is beyond the canopies over the wharf and behind that is Ravens Lane Bridge (No.142).

Opposite above: Berkhamsted Bottom Lock (No.55), *c*.1920. The lock is situated alongside the very cosy canalside public house, the Rising Sun, whose main entrance is from the towpath. It is a fairly shallow lock, with water cascading over the bottom gates. One balance beam is white, the other a dark colour. The river Bulbourne flows in behind the lock at this point, which is why the fisherman below the lock has his back to us.

Opposite below: The Crystal Palace Public House and canal, Berkhamsted, *c*.1960. This more recent postcard view is worth comparing with the picture on this page which was taken about fifty years earlier. The public house has lost its decorative 'Crystal Palace' frontage. The fence by the towpath now has trees growing and motor cars parked beside it, instead of the two bicycles leaning against the front wall of the pub in the older picture. The small building to the left of the pub has been demolished and the roadway now appears to run along there. Several pleasure craft – narrowboats, and cruisers – are moored by the towpath. (Judges Ltd)

The Canal and Station, Berkhamsted

Above: Broadwater Lock (No.53), Berkhamsted, 1908. A pair of northbound horse-drawn boats are waiting in the lock; both are sheeted up and travelling breasted up (side by side). A boatwoman is standing between the cabin doors of the nearer barge, with a child in her arms. A girl is standing on the lockside by the cabin and a boatman is towards the front of the boat. The towing line from the topmast has washing hanging from it. The figure standing by the balance beam of the bottom gate is probably just a passer by. Across the football field the end of Berkhamsted station platform and signals can be seen. Behind the goalposts is a row of goods wagons, possibly for Berkhamsted Gas Works, which had a branch line that ran down under the main line to the gasworks and canal.

Opposite above: Berkhamsted station and canal, *c.*1906. A pair of northbound narrowboats both have side cloths drawn up. The butty is using running blocks for towrope. The figures of two boys are on the towpath, and behind them is 'The Moor', Berkhamsted. Berkhamsted station is on the other side of the canal. A few wagons can be seen in the siding above high brick wall. A pedal carriage is passing on the road below. This scene is viewed from Castle Street Bridge (No.141).

Opposite below: Railway station and canal at Berkhamsted, *c.*1910. This is similar to the postcard view above, but shows more details of the station. The towpath and canal are quiet, and there are no people or boats in sight. Once again several goods wagons can be seen above the high brick wall in the sidings. The gap in the wall is where Brownlow Road leaves Station Road, passing under the railway.

CANAL, BERKHAMSTED.   K.983.

Above: Grand Junction Canal at Berkhamsted, 1951. The large trees on the right of the canal now completely hide the railway station, apart from the point where the canal turns. Some station buildings and a chimney rise up above tree tops. The wide towpath is now replaced by a track in the grass, and 'The Moor' can hardly been seen. Two men are standing under one of the large horse chestnut trees, and a very small cruiser is moored to the canal bank.

Right: Grand Junction Canal, Berkhamsted, *c.*1950. The picture is taken from 'The Moor' towards Lower Kings Road Bridge and Broadwater Lock. The office building on the offside between the tall trees was formerly Knowles mill buildings. A man is with a dog and boy, fishing from the towpath. (Judges Ltd)

Tring canal and railway cuttings through the Chiltern Hills, 1907. The top half of this postcard shows the 1½ mile long Tring canal cutting, which was constructed over two hundred years ago. Several canal boats loaded with coal are being pulled by horse from the towpath. Station Road Bridge (No.135) is in the distance. The slightly more modern and wider railway cutting at Tring is below, with a LNWR steam locomotive hauling a train past a lowered semaphore signal.

Tring summit level cutting near Tring, *c.*1980. The passenger narrow boat *Grebe* is cruising through Tring cutting with people on board. Behind the boat is Marshcroft Lane Bridge (No.134), which spans the middle of this 1½ mile long cutting. It is also a turnover bridge, hence the reason for the towpath climbing up towards the bridge. The road crossing this bridge is 22ft above the water. The cutting was originally dug out at 30ft, but with the spoil deposited on the top, it is probably a lot deeper than that. (Precision Photo Ltd)

Bulbourne maintenance yard, Bulbourne, near Tring, *c.*1970. The maintenance yard buildings were constructed for the Grand Junction Canal Co. during the late nineteenth and early twentieth centuries. They were mainly the work of Gordon Thomas, the company's Chief Engineer at that time. A pair of empty Murrells boats are moored in the foreground. The butty is on the right with its name slightly obscured. It could possibly be *Bingley*. (British Waterways)

Marsworth Top Lock (No.45) & Dry Dock, *c.1960*. A pair of empty narrowboats leaving the lock to start their downhill descent from Tring Summit. Stands are in place but there are no top planks; headlamps are mounted on the cratches of both boats; and the lock wheeler's bike is fixed to the front of the motor's cabin, behind the steerer holding the tiller. The building alongside the lock is a dry dock, originally built as part of a scheme to double all the Marsworth Locks, which was abandoned at a later date. (J. Salmon Ltd)

Marsworth Junction, *c.1940*. A Harvey-Taylor motor, *Roger,* is heading south, and is viewed from Watery Lane / Church Lane Bridge (No.131). The yard on the right is now British Waterways – Grand Union (south) yard and offices. The main line of the canal turns to the left, and the Aylesbury Branch heads off to the right behind buildings in the yard. (See Chapter 10 for the Aylesbury Arm.) For a later picture of *Roger* in Blue Line livery see the foot of page 25.

Vicarage Road Bridge (No.130) at Marsworth, *c*.1970. This nice spring scene shows the blossom outside The Ship at Marsworth. A pleasure boat is moored on the offside beyond a whitewashed bridge. Just to the left of the bridge is the popular Red Lion public house.

The Ship stores, Marsworth, *c*.1970. Here is a reverse view from that seen in the picture above, taken from the bridge looking back to the stores. Once again there are trees with blossom by the towpath. There is a nice view of the Old Ship stores with its thatched roof, and a swan swimming gracefully in the canal.

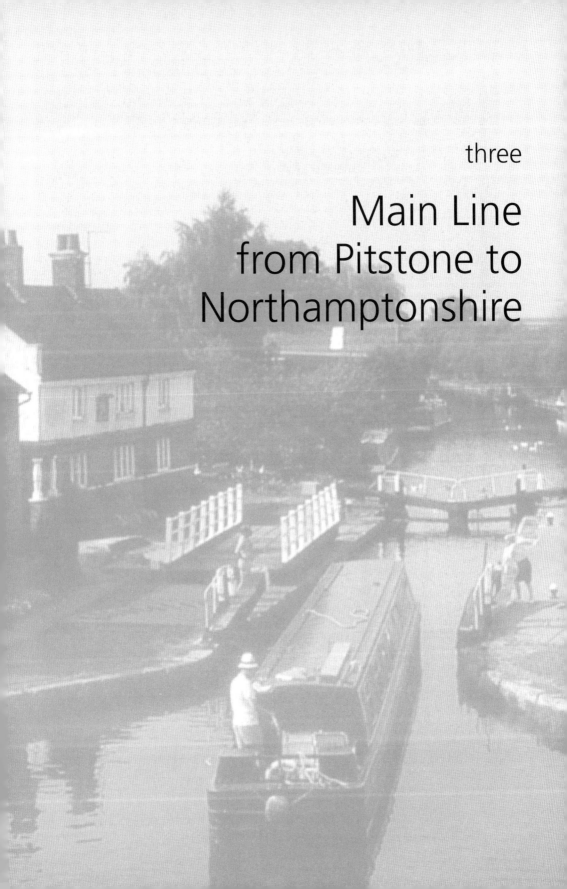

three

Main Line
from Pitstone to
Northamptonshire

Wintry scene at Slapton Lock (No.30), looking north from Slapton Bridge (No.120). A row of pleasure narrowboats are moored alongside the towpath above Slapton Lock, frozen in by thick ice. At this point, the canal has started its descent from the Chiltern Hills, into the vale of Aylesbury. The flat landscape of the vale can be seen in this winter view. (Mrs D. Westlake, Slapton W.I.)

Grand Junction Canal, Leighton Buzzard. This shows Wyvern Shipping's base with the passenger trip boat *Leighton Lady* moored in the foreground. Behind her are more boats and a covered wet/dry dock. This boatyard stands on the site once occupied by L.B. Faulkner, boat builder and canal carrier. (Photo: A.A. Catlin)

The Martins, Linslade, Leighton Buzzard, 1916. This very imposing house was in Linslade to the north of Leighton Buzzard, and has what appears to be a small boat dock for rowing boats. Rowing boats can be seen in the canal at the foot of the grounds to this house, with a couple of smartly dressed men wearing boaters in one of them. In the distance the balance beams can just be made out on the top gates of Leighton Lock (No.27). A man is fishing from a bank, and the thin black line of his fishing rod is visible against the white balance beams.

Near The Globe public house which is really part of Old Linslade, Leighton Buzzard, c.1910. A peaceful rural scene shows very woody surroundings and a man in a rowing boat with a small sail. There is a path on both banks of the canal, although the right hand path lined with telegraph poles is the proper towpath.

The Canal, Old Linslade

Three Locks, near Linslade.

Above: Three Locks, Soulbury, near Stoke Hammond, *c*.1940. This image is looking down the flight of three locks (Nos 24 to 26) at Soulbury, showing the side ponds alongside each of the locks. The buildings of The Three Locks public house are partly hidden behind the white building, which is the lock cottage. The black and white markings on the lock and lock equipment can be clearly seen. The large building on the right behind the three figures is one of the northern engine houses, which would have originally housed a steam engine. Nine of these engine houses were completed by 1841, between Marsworth and Fenny Stratford to pump lockage water from the Ouse Valley back to the reservoirs at Summit. (Photo: Carol Gibbs)

Opposite above: Old Linslade looking south, 1916. A high vantage point view of Stoke Road looks down on the canal below, and there is a road fence in the foreground. Bridge No.111 has a white open style parapet. Two figures are standing a little further along the towpath outside The Globe public house, which seems a little smaller then the present day premises. Above the trees are the roof tops and chimneys of Leighton Buzzard.

Opposite below: Old Linslade looking north, *c* 1910. This picture was taken from the same place as the previous photograph, but is looking in the opposite direction. The old LNWR railway main line from Euston has just left the tunnel under the road seen in the last photograph. This road is now out of sight behind the railway lines. The canal is turning away to the right where it almost encircles the village of Old Linslade which is hidden by the trees. On the right, there appears to be a large lake behind the towpath and trees which is where the river Ouzel flows. This lake was possibly caused by flooding after a spell of heavy rainfall.

Soulbury

Above: Three Locks, Soulbury, near Stoke Hammond, *c.*1960. There are a pair of Birmingham & Midland Canal Carriers; the butty is *Pictor* and the motor is possibly *Tadworth*, both in the top lock preparing to descend the flight. Two crew members can be seen on the boats whilst a third is busy raising the paddles to empty the lock of water. Both boats are empty; the upright stands and topmast are in place, but the top planks are lying in the hold of the boat. The white lock cottage for the flight is to the left of the middle lock, with the Three Locks pub below it beside the bottom lock. Unlike the previous picture on page 65, the side ponds are very weedy and overgrown, and are obviously out of use as they still are today.
(J. Salmon Ltd)

Left: Three Locks, Soulbury, near Stoke Hammond, 1960. The Willow Wren pair are *Dipper* the motor and *Cygnus* the butty, which have been steered into the lock by George Harris, ready to ascend. Both boats are laden with coal. The top planks are lying on top of the cargo, although the stands (uprights) and topmast are in place. Headlamps are mounted on the cratch of both boats.

Fenny Stratford, Bletchley, 1923. It is difficult to locate this scene, as a lot of building has taken place around here in recent years. This is probably Water Eaton Bridge (No.98). There was a wharf here which can be seen below the whitewashed bridge on the offside next to the large building. Beyond the bridge are more buildings which are part of the village of Water Eaton. The head of a figure can be seen looking over the middle of the bridge parapet.

Fenny Stratford, Bletchley, 1923. A pair of horse-drawn narrowboats are possibly just south of Fenny Stratford near Bridge No.97 at Water Eaton. There are a pair of horses pulling these boats which can just be seen between the bridge and second telegraph pole, with a man on the towpath walking behind them. Steerers are at the tillers of both boats, although the nearer boat is well out of water. Two children are standing on the offside of the canal beyond the nearer boat.

Grand Junction Canal, near Bletchley, *c.*1960. A pair of Willow Wren narrow boats are heading south; both are loaded and sheeted up. The motor *Curlew* is pulling an unidentified butty, which is on the other side of the bridge hole. The steerers of both boats are being watched as they pass by a figure looking over a fence to the left of the bridge parapet. For another view of *Curlew* see the top of page 13. (J. Salmon Ltd.)

Fenny Stratford Lock (No.22). This is an unusual lock in that it only has a fall of 12in. It was originally constructed to cure the problems of water leakage in the two-mile pound above Fenny Stratford. To the left is a row of old canal-side cottages, and behind them is the Red Lion public house with the white upper storey. There is a typical white Grand Junction lock cottage on the right, and hidden behind it is one of the northern engine houses. This lock also has a swing bridge across the lock chamber to allow vehicle access to the lock cottage. In this picture it is in open position, to the left of the bows of the boat entering the lock.

This view is near Simpson, *c*.1930, before it became part of present day Milton Keynes. It is a peaceful view of the canal and towpath lined with telegraph poles. A nice cottage is on the opposite side, with a footpath leading from the edge of the canal to the front door. A large greenhouse is alongside the cottage.

Bowlers Bridge (No.91) at Simpson, Milton Keynes. A more modern view of Simpson than the one above, since when it has become part of the Milton Keynes development. A nice wintry scene, with the new housing in the background on the other side of the canal. (Milton Keynes Development Corporation)

Above: Wolverton Aqueduct, Cosgrove, *c.*1940. This is the same as the previous picture at the foot of page 70, but is taken from below Wolverton iron trunk aqueduct. It shows the river Great Ouse and the embankment taking the canal onto the aqueduct. When the canal was first opened it crossed the river on the level and boats had to lock down to the river, cross it, and lock up other side. This involved a total of nine locks, which could not be used at times of flooding on the river. It was superseded by an aqueduct in 1805, which collapsed in 1808. The present iron trunk aqueduct was the work of Benjamin Bevan and was opened in 1811. (Philip Griffiths)

Opposite above: Grand Junction Canal at Old Wolverton, 1990. This view is looking south towards Galleon Bridge (No.68). Immediately to the right of the bridge on the canal side is The Galleon public house. The southern approach to the Wolverton Aqueduct would be behind the photographer. (Mrs S. Stone, New Manor W.I.)

Opposite below: Wolverton Aqueduct, Cosgrove, *c.*1960. A southbound pair of British Waterways narrow boats are crossing the aqueduct which spans the river Great Ouse. The unidentified motor is towing a former Grand Union Canal Carrying Co. butty *Toucan*, which is shown here in incomplete British Waterways livery. Roses and castles can be seen on the cabin doors by the steerer, and there is Turks Head ropework at the top of the rudder post. Both boats are obviously loaded as they have their side cloths drawn up. The fence on the canal side of the aqueduct towpath looks as though it has had some temporary repairs made to it. Galleons Bridge is in the distance (see above). (J. Salmon Ltd)

Cosgrove Lock (No.21), Cosgrove, *c*.1910. This old view shows an open swing bridge on the offside of the lock. This bridge was used to gain access to the towpath of the Old Stratford and Buckingham Arm, which ran along the south side of the arm. There are only ground paddles by the top gates, possibly because this is a shallow lock with a fall of only 3ft4in. The lock number plate is fastened on the whitewashed part of the balance beam.

Cosgrove Lock, Cosgrove, *c*.1970. This is a more modern view of the lock than in the picture above, and is taken from the other end of lock. A Union Canal Carriers motor *Birmingham* has just entered the lock and is heading south, loaded with coal. The beginning of the Stratford/Buckingham Arm is to the left behind the board with a lifebelt, and the trip boat *Linda* is in the background.

four

Stoke
Bruerne

Above: Stoke Bruerne Flight, Lock No.15, 1986. Beyond the lock is a twin arched bridge, No.53, and beyond that is the Stoke Bruerne Top Lock. The tops of the canal museum buildings and cottages are over the bridge parapet. In 1835 work began on duplicating the locks between Stoke Bruerne and Marsworth, because of the increase in traffic. This meant rebuilding or extending existing bridges that crossed the tail of locks, and also building an additional lock chamber alongside the existing one. By the time the construction work got underway there was a fall in traffic, and the scheme was abandoned. The two-arched bridges remained with water access under one arch only, and the duplicate locks that were built were later filled in, except at Stoke Bruerne which was re-excavated at a more recent date.

Opposite above: Lock No.19 on Stoke Bruerne Flight, *c.*1970. One of the first hotel boats on the system, the horse-drawn narrowboat *Pamela,* has just left lock 19 and is about to enter Stoke Bruerne Bottom Lock (No.20). The lock cottage is beside the upper lock. Coloured bobbins can be seen on the horse harness. The bottom lock is ready with the gates open. There are raised brick blocks to put one's feet against when pushing the lock gates closed or open. (Photograph: A. Chamberlain)

Opposite below: Aerial view of the canal and the village of Stoke Bruerne. The canal curves through the middle of the village. The top of lock No.15 is just visible at the bottom of the picture and the double arched bridge is above this. Only the left-hand arch can be seen, as trees are obscuring the other arch. Above this is the Stoke Bruerne Top Lock (No.14). Only the right-hand chamber can be used. The Boat Inn is to the left and the canal museum buildings are opposite, to the right. The canal is seen turning away to the right and at the top of the picture on the left is the southern portal of Blisworth Tunnel. (Aerial photograph by Photoair)

Above: Stoke Bruerne Top Lock, *c*.1970. A pair of narrow boats in the top lock, loaded with packages or possibly short lengths of timber. The skipper of the boat is standing by top gates talking to a taller man dressed in a suit, another person is to the left on the island between the two locks. To the left is the Boat Inn with stable block, to the right canal cottages, and behind them, the Waterways Museum formerly a mill. Moored outside the museum is a Fellows, Morton & Clayton horse-drawn boat, probably *Northwich*.

Opposite above: Stoke Bruerne Top Lock (No.14), 1970. A pair of empty working narrowboats are about to leave the lock; the butty is on the left and motor is on the right. A number of spectators are watching the boats on what looks like a cold winter's day. Just over the bridge parapet is lock No.15; the reverse view can be seen on page 75. The lock to the right was originally built as part of the duplicating programme, and here has a canal weighing machine installed with an old Fellows, Morton & Clayton butty in the machine. (Beric Tempest)

Opposite below: The Boat Inn, Stoke Bruerne, 1980. A pleasant canal-side public house with a thatched roof is just above Stoke Bruerne top lock (in the foreground of the picture). This pub was modernised internally in the 1960s, along with the old stable block, which was turned into tea rooms.

Left: Stoke Bruerne Top Lock, 1972. A loaded narrowboat is entering the top lock and is managing to squeeze through with only one of the top gates open. A family with children are watching from the side of the lock, and there are two nice old wooden bollards on the left-hand side of the lock. The Waterways Museum building looks very clean and tidy, as though it has had some work carried out on the exterior. (J. Arthur Dixon)

Below: Stoke Bruerne. This is a drawing of a pair of Grand Union Canal Carrying Co. narrowboats: the butty *Moon* is on the right with an unidentified motor on the left. The boats appear to be breasted up as the tiller on the butty has been removed. The drawing shows the ropework and painted decoration on the butty rudder post. The waterway museum buildings and canal side cottages are in the background. (Drawn by Robert Wilson)

Stoke Bruerne Top Lock (No.14), 1980. Here is a busy scene which is more typical of the present day. Two pleasure boats are leaving the lock, and many more boats are moored on both sides of the canal. Crowds of visitors are everywhere; some are along the towpath on their way to the waterways museum and some are crossing the lock to The Boat Inn. (J. Salmon Ltd)

Stoke Bruerne Top Lock, 1990. A working narrowboat loaded with coal is in the top lock waiting to descend. The colourful decoration can be seen on the cratch, and the side cloths are partly drawn up. The top planks are in place and the top mast is extended, although this motor appears to be travelling alone and not towing. The canal-side cottages are to the left, and below them is modern local housing. (Mr S.Fitch – Yardley Gobion W.I.)

Stoke Bruerne, June 1971. A pair of working narrowboats belonging to Union Canal Carriers are moored above Stoke Bruerne. The roof of the waterways museum can be seen in the background beyond the left-hand boat and towpath. The boat moored on the inside is the butty *Moon* and was formerly part of the Grand Union Canal Carrying Co. fleet; it is a Small Woolwich built by Harland & Wolff in 1935. The motor *Petrel* moored on the outside is a former Fellows, Morton & Clayton boat. This picture clearly shows the difference between a butty and a motor when seen from the stern. The butty cabin is not as tall as the motors; the stern of the butty curves upward whereas the motor's counter is flatter, sitting down in the water so the propeller has plenty of water to push through when moving. There is decorative paintwork on both boats' tillers, and the motor has a large fender on the stern, whilst there is decorative ropework on the butty's rudder post – the Turks Head and Swan's Neck. (Photograph: D. Miller)

five

Between the Tunnels (Blisworth to Braunston)

Blisworth Tunnel, southern portal, 1980. A working narrow boat is leaving the southern end of the 3,056-yard long Blisworth Tunnel. When the tunnel was completed in 1805 it had no towpath, and all boats had to be legged through. The building to the right of the tunnel portal is the old leggers' hut, and these men would hire themselves out to leg boats through the tunnel. (Beric Tempest)

Blisworth Tunnel, northern end, 1968. A pair of Blue Line Boats are pictured here. The motor *Nutfield* and the butty *Raymond* are on their way from Atherstone, loaded with coal for Jam 'Ole at Southall, and are about to enter the northern end of the tunnel. The butty's side cloths are drawn up to the top planks. Roses and castles decorate the open cabin doors, and there is decorative ropework on the butty's rudder post. The sign by the tunnel entrance states 'Keep Right'. (Robert Wilson)

The re-opening of the Blisworth Tunnel in 1984. The tunnel caused many problems during its construction and was the last section of the canal to be completed. There had been several short term closures and eventually in 1980 it was closed for extensive reconstruction and repairs. This postcard was issued to celebrate the re-opening on 22 August 1984. As can be seen, crowds of people and boats were present at this important occasion (G. Freeston)

The re-opening of the Blisworth Tunnel in 1984 – the reverse of the previous picture. All the officials and media are on board the first two boats to enter the tunnel after the re-opening, which was carried out by Sir Leslie Young CBE, DL, Chairman of British Waterways Board at that time. (G. Freeston)

Above: High House Bridge (No.29), 1971. Union Canal Carriers motor boat *Petrel is* pushing its way through the ice on Boxing Day 1971, loaded with coal for Berkhamsted. There are two figures standing on the bow, probably to warn the steerer of any thick ice ahead; the side cloths are half drawn up and have already collected a lot of snow. The steerer is well wrapped up in a heavy coat and with a cap on his head. It is just possible to see the decorated water cans and mop on the cabin roof between the engine exhaust and stove chimneys. (Robert Wilson)

Opposite above: Weedon, Northamptonshire, *c.*1950. This is a Thomas Clayton (Oldbury) Ltd tank boat. Storage tanks for holding bulk liquids, like tar, were underneath its flat boarded deck. The canal here at Weedon crosses the river Nene and the village on a high embankment, splitting the village in two. This picture was taken at one end of the embankment and the roofs and chimneys of the village can be seen over the distant towpath hedge.

Opposite below: Long Buckby wharf and cottages, *c.*1980. Here is a view of Anchor Cottage, seen from Lock No.8 of Buckby Flight. One of the balance beams of the top gate is in the foreground with the ground paddle behind. One of the cottages is a small canal side shop and store, which the signboards on the towpath outside state is 'Open for business so why not moor and shop'. (Photograph: Brian D. Palmer)

Long Buckby, 1975. Ex-Fellows, Morton & Clayton motor boat *Jaguar* is heading south under the bridge loaded with coal, and is sitting well down in the water. The roses and castles and lozenge-shape decorations can be seen on the triangular cratch at the front, alongside the headlamp. The side cloths are partly drawn up. The top mast is extended, although no towing is taking place. The white shirt of the steerer can just be made out in the gloom below the bridge hole. (Robert Wilson)

Buckby Top Lock and cottage, *c.*1980. This is a drawing of what used to be Ginger's Canal Stores in the top lock cottage. There is an advertising board outside the cottage on the towpath. The top lock and handrails for the balance beams of the bottom gates are in the foreground. The bow of the narrowboat is above the top gates.

Right: Narrowboats above Buckby Top Lock, *c.*1980. The butty *Hyades* above the top lock was built in 1935 by Harland & Wolff and is a Star Class boat, a Small Woolwich. Beyond the lock is Watling Street Bridge (No.11) which carries the busy A5 trunk road across the canal at this point. The distant cottage by the trees is actually alongside the road, not the canal.

Below: The Old Toll House, Norton Junction, 1980. This toll house is situated at the junction with the Old Union Canal (now part of the Leicester line of the Grand Union Canal). This watercolour picture shows the old toll house between the trees, now used as a holiday cottage. The Grand Junction Canal passes under the bridge (no.10) to the left of the toll house. The entrance to the Old Union Canals is on the right. (Watercolour by Garth Allan)

Hyades, seen at Long Buckby Top Lock

Eastern portal of the Braunston Tunnel, 1980. A pleasure narrowboat is about to enter the tunnel which is 2,048 yards long. Unlike Blisworth, Braunston Tunnel caused no real problems to William Jessop's engineers, and opened as scheduled in 1796. However, there was a minor blunder when two of the contractors set off on different bearings, resulting in a kink in the tunnel about 400 yards from the eastern end. The towpath in the tunnel cuttings can be eroded in places, although it looks in good condition in this picture. (Photograph: Douglas M. Smith)

six

Braunston

Above: Nelson Lock (No.3) at Braunston, *c.*1980. A pair of pleasure boats are about to leave Nelson Lock: an Anglo-Welsh narrowboat and a GRP Cruiser. The top gates are open, ready for the climb up the rest of the Braunston Flight. Nelson Bridge (No.4) is over the tail of the lock, and the white building to its right is the Admiral Nelson Inn with a cottage alongside. Above the bridge parapet some buildings can be seen in the village of Braunston. (J. Salmon Ltd)

Right: Nelson Lock, Braunston Flight, Braunston, 1966. George Wain is taking the motor *Nuneaton* and the butty *Alperton* out of Nelson Lock, Braunston. They are loaded with tamarinds from London Docks for HP sauce in Birmingham. The view is taken from the bridge and looks down on cabin tops. It shows roses and castles decoration on water cans, and also a mop on the motor cabin top. There are brass rings on chimneys and decorative ropework on the butty rudder post. (Photograph: Mike Webb)

Above: Nelson Bridge (No.4) and Nelson Lock (No.3), Braunston, *c.*1960. Blue Line Carriers butty *Lucy* is passing under Nelson bridge on her way into the lock, loaded with coal from Atherstone for Jam 'Ole at Southall. Bill Whitlock is the captain of this pair and is getting ready to close the bottom gates. Two women are steering the boats. (Photograph: Robert Wilson)

Right: Braunston Bottom Lock (No.1), *c.*1960. These are a Blue Line Carriers pair of boats. The motor, *Renfrew,* and the butty, *Lucy,* are in Braunston Bottom, getting ready to start the climb up this flight of six locks. There is an old wooden bollard in the foreground, and on the other side of the lock where a boatwoman is preparing to slow the butty's progress by running the rope around the bollard. The decoration on the cabin can be seen clearly, as can some of the coal in the butty. The lock cottage in the background is now a canal-side shop. (Robert Wilson)

Left: Bottom Lock (No.1) Braunston Flight, Braunston. 1983. A traditionally styled narrowboat is leaving the lock and passing under Bottom Lock Bridge (No.2). It is heading towards Braunston boatyard, where many boats are moored beyond the bridge hole. Roofs of buildings can be seen over the bridge parapet. (Photograph: Patrick Thom)

Below: Braunston Yard, Braunston, *c.*1960. Mrs Sydney McDonald and her family are on board a pair of ex-BWB boats, being used by Willow Wren. The motor is *Tarporley*, but the butty is unknown. Smoke is coming out of the butty's stove chimney. There is a plastic cover over the top of *Tarpoley's* chimney, to protect the nicely polished brass rings. A large wheel can be seen inside *Tarpoley's* cabin, to control engine speed. (Photograph: Robert Wilson)

Grand Junction Canal at Braunston, *c.*1970. Here are a pair of Blue Line Canal Carriers boats. The butty *Raymond* is being towed by an unknown motor, which is possibly *Roger*. The butty has its side cloths drawn up but the motor has not. They are heading east towards Braunston Yard, where many narrowboats can be seen in the distance, and beyond them is Bottom Lock Bridge (No.2). On the right is a wooden footbridge taking the towpath over one of the entrances to Braunston Marina. Beyond the footbridge is the chimney to the pumping station, which was built by the Grand Junction Canal Co. for returning lockage water up to the tunnel summit.

Blue Line Bridge, Braunston Marina. This elegant Horseley Ironworks bridge crossed part of the original line of the Oxford canal before it was straightened out during Telford's improvements of the 1830s. The marina was originally formed out of two small reservoirs. These were established by the Grand Junction Canal Co. as a safeguard for their water let down the Braunston Flight of locks, although most of it was back pumped. The flats and houses on the south side of the marina were built fairly recently. (J. Salmon Ltd)

Grand Junction Canal at Braunston, *c.*1960. A pair of Blue Line Canal Carriers boats, *Roger* and *Raymond,* are moored below one of the Horseley iron bridges. The white wing wall of the bridge can be seen in the bottom left corner of the picture. The old toll house is beyond the boats. A line of moored craft is leading towards Butchers Bridge. This section of the canal was originally part of the Oxford canal, which is now part of Grand Union Canal. (J. Salmon Ltd)

Working narrowboats at Braunston. On the outside of the picture is a former Fellows, Morton & Clayton butty *Australia.* A pair of former Grand Union Canal Carrying Co. boats are on the inside. These are *Angel* and *Aldgate,* which were paired whilst working for that company. Both are Town Class boats which were built by Harland & Wolff in 1936, and registered at Coventry. They are both Large Woolwich boats. In this picture they are painted in British Waterways Board's blue and yellow livery. (Photograph: Heather Copping/IWA)

seven

Paddington
Arm

Grand Junction Canal Basin at Paddington. This is an early picture of the basin at Paddington, probably just after it was opened in 1801. There are trees and rural landscape beyond the warehouses. A barge is at the nearer end of the basin, unloading part of its cargo into a cart. Other barges are surrounding the basin, and many interested people are strolling around the basin. (British Waterways)

Little Venice, Paddington, c.1910. This was once a busy canal area, but there are no boats in this old view. The large, very grand houses which are partly hidden behind the trees on Paddington Island are no longer there, having been demolished and replaced by Rembrandt Gardens. The Harrow Road Bridge (No.2) with white outline around the bridge hole is the entrance to Paddington basin.

Little Venice, Paddington, 1937. This is almost identical to the previous picture, but is looking to the right of the bridge. Harrow Road Bridge (No.2) has been rebuilt with a flat deck. Immediately to its right, above a high brick wall and alongside the towpath, is Beauchamp Lodge, which was built in about 1854, and is now used as a community centre. There are a couple of barges moored to the island and the large house beyond can be seen more clearly in this view than the last.

Little Venice, Paddington, c.1970. This is Terrace Bridge at Westbourne and there is a horse-bridge with an early type of trip boat moored to the left. The white building partly hidden behind the bridge is the Bridge House pub. When not in Venice, the poet Robert Browning lived in a house near here. He is supposed to have given this large area of water the name 'Little Venice', because it reminded him of Venice. It is also known as Browning's Pool. (Paddington Waterways Society)

View west from the old toll house, now British Waterways Office, Grand Junction Canal, Paddington, *c*.1970. An assortment of boats are moored along the offside of the canal. The houses in Blomfield Road are behind the boats, and a group of children are playing on the towpath on the left. The Formosa Street footbridge was erected by Paddington Council in 1914, but has since been demolished and replaced by a new modern bridge. (Paddington Waterways Society)

Grand Junction Canal, Paddington, *c*.1970. Here is an almost identical view to the previous picture, but it is taken from the opposite side of the canal. The modern flats in Delamere Terrace are behind the towpath, where a lone boat is moored. Formosa Street footbridge is in the distance. The spire behind the trees belongs to St Mary Magdalene's church, which was built in 1873 and designed by Street. (Paddington Waterways Society)

Carlton Bridge (No.4), Westbourne Park, 1999. This painting shows the bridge that takes Great Western Road across the Paddington branch of the canal. It takes its name from the Carlton Bridge Tavern which is the white building alongside the bridge. The tavern was rebuilt in the mid 1980s. (Painting by Jonathon Phipps)

Acton Lane Bridge (No.9), Harlesden, c.1910. The building to the left is the Grand Junction Arms public house which is still there today, and obviously takes its name from the canal. This canal bridge was replaced in the 1920s with a more modern flat deck bridge, which is still there. A rowing boat with several people in it is beneath the bridge, and Harlesden power station is beyond the bridge. A narrowboat is being loaded with ash from a chute.

Above: North Circular Road Aqueduct, Stonebridge Park, *c.*1920. Three west London boroughs, Paddington, Marylebone & Kensington, used to barge their refuse out by canal. It was used to infill the large holes in the worked-out brickfields in Hayes and Yeading. The St Marylebone borough council tug *Tyburn* is probably towing a string of refuse barges, although only the bows of the leading one can be seen. This aqueduct was constructed in the early 1920s to span the North Circular Road, which was built as part of the development of Wembley Stadium for the British Empire Exhibition of 1924. This aqueduct was demolished recently and rebuilt to accommodate the widening of the road below, from two lanes each way to four.

Opposite above: Grand Junction Canal near Park Royal, *c.*1910. This view is looking west from near Abbey Road, when this area was still open countryside. During the First World War, munitions factories were opened here. After the war, Heinz, Guinness and McVities moved into the Park Royal industrial estate, and they all made use of the canal. Later, various housing estates sprang up and the whole area has now been fully developed.

Opposite below: Grand Junction Canal at Alperton, *c.*1910. This is the view west from opposite the Pleasure Boat public house and near the Ealing Road bridge. In the distance is Piggery Bridge (No.12), Alperton, that now carries Manor Farm Road. The bridge was widened and rebuilt in recent years. Alperton wharf is to the right, and there is now a large Sainsbury's supermarket to the left behind the towpath.

CANAL BRIDGE, HORSENDEN LANE, GREENFORD.

Above: Ballot Box Bridge, Horsenden Lane, Perivale, *c.*1920. Many school children are fishing and playing by the canal. They are all under the watchful eye of the local policeman, whose silhouette can be seen over the middle of the bridge parapet. There are three tie rods fixed to the face of the bridge to reinforce it. These all carry the initials of the Grand Junction Canal Co. and the date 1909. A small wharf used to be on the left by the fenced road. Horsenden Lane leads up to Horsenden Hill and the Ballot Box public house. The hill and surrounding woods are a small part of the ancient Middlesex forest, and the walk to the top of the hill still affords lovely views over parts of Middlesex. The Ballot Box pub used to be nearer the canal, and was where boat people were able to cast their votes at the time of an election, hence the name of the pub.

Opposite above: Ballot Box Bridge (No.13), Perivale. 1911. This is the view south across the top of the canal bridge. The local policeman and postman are standing on the bridge. Behind the policeman the finger post reads 'Public Footpath to Horsenden Hill'. is A diamond–shaped weight restriction sign is inside the left-hand parapet, on the far side of the bridge, and there are tie rods on the outer face of the bridge.

Opposite below: The Grand Junction Canal, Paddington Branch at Northolt, 1975. T. & D. Murrell's motor barge *Cadellis* is pictured here with a couple of dumb barges in tow. The view is taken from Kensington Road Bridge (No.17) at Northolt. This area around the canal is still fairly rural and a lot of rubbish infill took place between the world wars, although the modern housing of Smith's Farm Estate is visible just behind the trees.

ALPERTON CANAL BRIDGE, ALPERTON.

J. H. & Co's Series

Bankside from Hayes Bridge, Southall, 1910. Although this does not show a wintry scene, this card carries the greeting 'A Happy Christmas', and shows a row of terraced houses called Bankside that are overlooking the canal. One of Southall's gasometers is in the distance, and a group of women are on the towpath in the middle distance. This scene has changed very little, except that Bankside is cluttered with parked cars, as most roads are today. The offside by the telegraph pole now has a large B&Q superstore, as well as a large Fiat car dealership.

Bull's Bridge Junction, Southall, c.1920. This is the point where the Paddington Arm joins the main line beyond the white canal bridge, and turns left to Brentford and right to Braunston. The toll house still stands virtually unaltered, as does the bridge. Beyond the bridge is the roof of a building which is no longer there. In more recent years there was a British Waterways yard, which has now been replaced by a canal-side Tesco superstore.

eight

Slough Arm

Cowley Peachey Junction, Cowley, 1985. Here is the towpath bridge at the junction of the main line and Slough Arm, which carries the towpath over to the arm. It is seen from the beginning of the branch, looking towards the junction. The towpath for the main canal passes straight across the picture. The approach to the branch slopes upwards behind the brick support wall, which allowed access for horses or people from either direction. This bridge with iron lattice railings probably dates from the opening of this branch in 1882.

Aqueduct over the Fray's river, Cowley Peachey, 1985. To pacify mill owners when the arm to Slough was built, the river crosses three waterways – Fray's river, River Colne and Colne brook – on three identical aqueducts, so as not to impede the flow of water in each of these watercourses. Each aqueduct consisted of an iron trough, with lattice railings and brick abutments.

Right: London coal duty marker alongside the canal bridge to Little Britain, 1985. This post originally indicated that any coal bound for London was liable for duty when it passed this marker. Eight years after the branch was built, the tax was abolished. The duty marker carries the arms of the city of London, and beneath this, the relevant number and chapter of the act that applies.

Below: St Mary's Road Bridge (Schools Bridge), Langley, *c.*1970. A pleasure narrowboat is passing under St Mary's Bridge, heading east towards Iver and the main line. The bridge is built on skew, and the traffic priority signs show that it is narrow. Modern industrial units at Langley are beyond the bridge. (Photograph: Martin Wood)

The view eastwards from the top of St Mary's Road Bridge, Slough Arm, at Langley, *c.*1970. A pair of pleasure narrow boats are heading towards Cowley Peachey Junction and the main line. The modern industrial units lining both sides of the canal are all fenced off, and have turned their backs on the canal, with the exception of the building beyond the boats on the towpath side, which still has a canopy hanging out over the canal. (Photograph: Martin Wood)

Wexham Road Bridge, Slough, c.1970. A converted working narrowboat is being used as a passenger trip boat, probably during the 1974 Slough canal rally. This is a typical canal bridge for this arm, but unfortunately has a rather unsightly pipe attached to this side of it.

Slough Arm of Grand Junction Canal, September 1974. A British Waterways traditional working narrowboat is towing the weedcutter *Wilder* to carry out clearance work on the channel of the arm prior to the 1974 Slough canal rally.

Slough Arm near Slough Basin, 1974. This picture was taken during the 1974 Slough canal protest rally. Both banks are lined with boats attending the event and many groups of people are walking along either side of the canal. (Avril Lansdell)

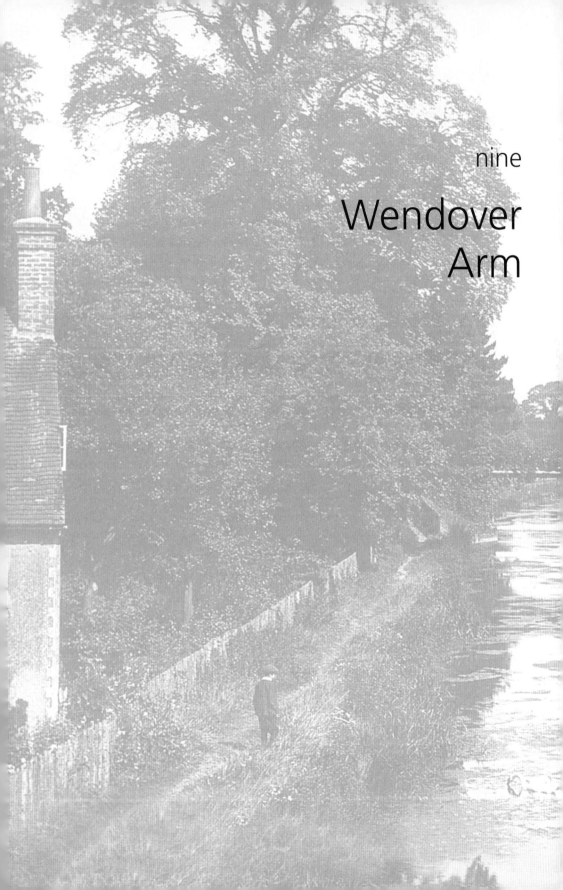

nine

Wendover
Arm

New Mill Bridge, Tring

Canal and Dockyard, New Mill, Tring.

Above: The Grand Junction Canal pumping station at Little Tring, 1908. This large pumping station was built in 1815 and started work in 1818 using steam engines. The buildings and engines survived in this form until 1927, when the chimney and upper storeys were demolished and the engines removed. The remaining single-storey pumping station was lengthened, and the windows were replaced by ones removed from the engine house at Foxton Inclined Plane. The stop lock in the foreground dates from around 1898, and was built as a final solution to the continual loss of water from the Wendover Arm beyond this point. The picture was taken a few years after the final abandonment of the branch for navigation. It was only being used as a water supply channel to the Tring reservoirs and the reeds had grown below the bottom gates, although the single paddle is still fixed to the nearside bottom gate.

Opposite above: Gamnel Bridge, New Mill near Tring, *c.*1910. Apart from the towpath bridge over the entrance to the Wendover Arm at Bulbourne Junction, this is the first bridge along the arm, and it is also a turnover bridge. The buildings to the right are part of Bushell Bros boat-building yard. A moored barge is in the foreground, and behind it is a heap of gravel or sand, with a wheelbarrow lying on its side. A very smartly dressed man wearing a boater is sitting on the bank by the towpath, looking at the mirror-like reflections of the bridge and buildings in the water.

Opposite below: Bushell Bros boat-building yard at New Mill near Tring, 1935. A pair of Harvey-Taylor boats are moored next to the yard. The motor is on the inside with smoke coming from its chimney. Both boats are empty with top planks in place. Various items are lying around the yard - an old wagon and a bicycle beside boats – a couple of butty tiller arms can be seen behind the covered dock. This is a reverse view of the previous picture.

Grand Junction canal reservoirs at Tring, 1911. The Wendover Arm was originally built as a feeder, then converted to a navigable branch feeding the Tring summit. Many reservoirs alongside the arm were built at different times to supply water to the Wendover Arm, and in turn the summit level. This view is of one of the reservoirs at Tring. A couple of men can be seen on the island between the two trees on the left, and there are also two figures in the water.

Tring reservoirs in winter, 1906. Some of the skaters have sticks as though they are playing a make shift game of ice hockey. A flight of swans are in the sky.

Eastern reservoir, Tring, *c*.1910. This view is probably of Tringford reservoir, which was originally built between 1814 and 1816. A small brick building with a tiled roof and chimney is on the left, and a larger wooden building is behind it. The top of a house is on the opposite side of the reservoir, above a clump of trees in the centre distance.

Marsworth reservoir, Tring, *c*.1930. The reservoir was originally opened in 1806. In this view the water levels seem to be low, as all the steep brick-lined walls around the reservoir are uncovered. A man and a boy are busy fishing on a tiny foreshore in the foreground. Behind them it seems as though steps were built into the reservoir wall.

GRAND JUNCTION CANAL, HALTON.

THE CANAL HALTON,

Above: The Canal at Halton, 1913. This postcard is produced by the same local photographer as the previous photograph, and is probably taken at the same time. It is a reverse view of the previous picture, and is taken from Halton Bridge looking east. The canal is in a similar state with reedy banks and patches of floating weed. The two swans with the youngster are still there, as is one of the boys who is standing on the opposite bank this time. The gate across this path is missing, but is shown in the next picture. In the middle distance between the tall trees, is the Rothschilds Bridge, covered with a growth of vegetation. The houses on either side of the canal are still there today and are virtually unaltered.

Opposite above: Hare Lane or Rothschilds Bridge at Halton, *c.*1916. With such a heavy growth of vegetation all over this bridge, it makes identification difficult. It is certainly not Halton Bridge as this is a turnover bridge. Stop planks have been inserted below the bridge, but left slightly open, as if only to restrict, not stop, the flow of water. There are three men standing on the towpath, two are in uniforms and are probably airmen from the nearby RFC camp at Halton.

Opposite below: Halton Bridge, Halton, *c.*1910. This bridge has also become overgrown with vegetation and the reeds are encroaching into the water channel of the canal. There are two swans swimming amongst the patches of floating weed, and the darker head of a young swan can be seen behind one of the adults. Two boys are standing by the towpath, and behind them are some of the houses in Halton village. This bridge was demolished in 1967.

WENDOVER, THE CANAL AT HALTON.

CANAL HALTON.

Above: Wendover branch canal at Halton, 1913. This is almost identical to the previous picture, but is taken to one side of Halton Bridge, and is in line with the towpath. Whilst it is postmarked in 1913 like the previous picture, it looks as though it may have been taken earlier, because the canal is clear of weed and reeds. Three boys are standing on the path by the gate. More can be seen of Rothchilds Bridge, which is still slightly overgrown with vegetation. The footpath on the offside rises up onto this bridge.

Left: Wendover Canal at Halton, *c.*1910. This is an unusual vertical outlook taken from a low view point. The decorative ironwork can be seen on this bridge in the foreground. Beyond that is Halton Bridge, which was demolished in the late 1960s. The canal appears to be relatively clear, although the water levels are low after the closure of navigation along this section of canal. The silhouette of a figure is standing on the towpath between the bridges.

The original Perch Bridge is seen from the north side where the canal makes a long turn towards Wendover, *c*.1900. This bridge was replaced shortly after this picture was taken. At the same time, the Golden Perch Inn, from which the bridge acquired its name, was demolished. The canal is fairly clear at this point. A man can be seen sitting in the foreground on the bank below the towpath.

Perch Bridge near Halton, *c*.1910. This shows an identical view to the previous picture, except that this one is taken a little nearer to the bridge. It shows the replacement bridge that was put up by Alfred de Rothschild. This bridge is still in existence today, although a little the worse for wear through constant use by modern traffic travelling along Halton Lane.

Above: Perch Bridge, Halton near Wendover, *c.*1900. Here is another view of the original bridge, but from the south side. A man with his arms crossed is resting against the parapet. Some parts of the parapet are damaged, with bricks missing, and vegetation is also taking hold of the structure. There is a semi-circular recess on the offside abutment above the water line, which is still there today on the replacement bridge.

Right: Grand Junction Canal near Wendover, *c.*1910. A smartly dressed man is fishing from the towpath opposite an area known as 'the wides'. Several small streams flow into the canal at the wides, and it was sufficiently wide for narrow boats to be able to turn when the canal was open to navigation. The channel of the canal looks clear, although reeds are growing along the towpath bank.

ten

Aylesbury
Arm

Osier Bed Lock (No.15), Aylesbury, c.1920. This is a pleasant rural setting on the edge of Aylesbury, which is now swallowed up in the 1970s factory developments. The lock would appear to be empty and the left hand gate paddle has been left open. Two men are standing beyond the balance beam on the offside of the canal, and beside them two women are sitting on the ground, dressed in white and wearing hats.

Osier Bed Lock (No.15) at Aylesbury, 1974. This is a reverse view of the previous picture, but is taken fifty years later. Some of the modern factory buildings are visible between the trees. The flat deck of Oakfield Bridge which carries Aylesbury ring road is in the distance to the left. A small brick parapet belonging to a tiny aqueduct is to the right of the lock by the towpath. This is where the Bear brook flows under the canal. (Judges Ltd)

The view towards Aylesbury from Park Street Lock (No.16), 1925. The rebuilt Park Street Bridge is beyond the lock. A lack of foliage on the trees suggests it is winter. There is a horse in the field on the right of the canal, although it is easier to see his reflection in the water, as the field appears rather dark.

Park Street Lock (No.16) at Aylesbury, c.1960. A working narrowboat is waiting above the lock, which is empty. The lock wheeler walking along the towpath has just reached the lock, and is ready to lift the paddles and fill the lock. There is a large building hidden amongst trees behind the towpath. (J. Salmon Ltd)

Park Street Bridge (No.17) and the Nestlé Factory, *c*.1900. This view shows the original canal bridge. The top picture on page 23 shows the replacement bridge. Behind the bridge is lock No.16. The factory to the right of the bridge dates from around 1870 and was originally part of Aylesbury Condensed Milk Co. Later it became part of Nestlé, alomg with the wharves below the bridge by the factory.

Aylesbury Canal Basin, *c*.1970. This is a busy scene with lots of moored narrowboats in the basin, including a working boat to the right. The view is looking east from the terminal basin towards a distant footbridge. On the left are some of the old warehouses that remain beside the canal. (Judges Ltd)

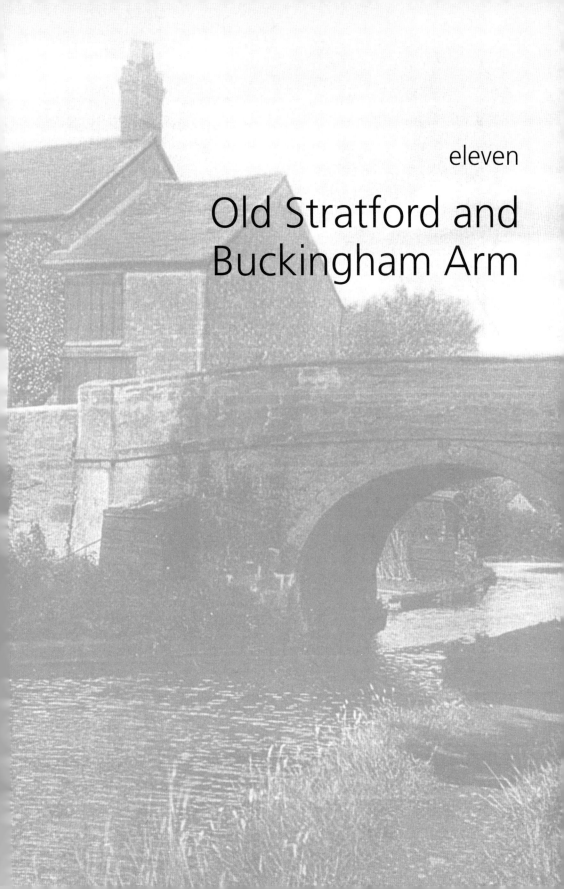

eleven

Old Stratford and Buckingham Arm

The Bridge, Buckingham Arm, Nr Wolverton.

CANAL AND DRAWBRIDGE, DEANSHANGER.

Above: Bridge No.9 and Deanshanger Wharf, *c.*1930. Alongside this bridge is the wharf house, adjoining part of the wharf buildings with a slightly lower roof line, and covered over loading bays above the roadway. Beyond the bridge, part of the wharf can be seen. The bridge appears to be built of stone, and the narrow dimensions of this branch are obvious when comparing the size of the bridge hole with the one on the top of page 126, which is on the Old Stratford branch and has wide dimensions. There are two very small wooden storage huts alongside the bridge, which are possibly too small for storing stop planks. (Philip Griffiths)

Opposite above: Bridge No.1 Old Stratford Arm near Cosgrove, 1916. This 1¼-mile long branch was built to wide dimensions, like the main line of the canal. This bridge was demolished in the 1970s, along with the second bridge a little further along the branch. The first 150 yards of canal are still in water up to the site of this bridge. (Philip Griffiths)

Opposite below: Drawbridge at Deanshanger on Buckingham Arm, *c.*1920. The nine-mile-long Buckingham Arm from Old Stratford was built to narrow dimensions. (Buckingham Canal Society)

Canal Bridge No.10 at Deanshanger, *c.*1920. This is another bridge in the same village. A cottage with a possibly thatched roof is standing to the right of the bridge some distance from the canal. A very neat set of steps with a handrail is leading to a footpath from the bridge, although the towpath is on the opposite side, where a boy is fishing. Once again the narrowness of the bridge hole can be seen. A diamond-shaped weight restriction sign is on top of the bridge by the steps. (Buckingham Canal Society)

Buckingham Arm near Deanshanger, *c.*1920. This very rural scene is difficult to identify, as it has no visible structures, except for the sharp left turn in the canal as it curves its way in a semi-circle around the edge of Deanshanger. (Buckingham Canal Society)